THE POETRY OF NITROGEN

The Poetry of Nitrogen

Walter the Educator™

SKB

Silent King Books a WhichHead Imprint

Copyright © 2023 by Walter the Educator™

All rights reserved. No part of this book may be reproduced in any manner whatsoever without written permission except in the case of brief quotations embodied in critical articles and reviews.

First Printing, 2023

Disclaimer
This book is a literary work; poems are not about specific persons, locations, situations, and/or circumstances unless mentioned in a historical context. This book is for entertainment and informational purposes only. The author and publisher offer this information without warranties expressed or implied. No matter the grounds, neither the author nor the publisher will be accountable for any losses, injuries, or other damages caused by the reader's use of this book. The use of this book acknowledges an understanding and acceptance of this disclaimer.

"Earning a degree in chemistry changed my life!"
- Walter the Educator

dedicated to all the chemistry lovers, like myself, across the world

CONTENTS

Dedication v

Why I Created This Book? 1

One - The Silent Hero 2

Two - Every Space 4

Three - Harmonious Ways 6

Four - Cosmic Embrace 8

Five - Proteins And DNA 10

Six - Oh, Nitrogen 12

Seven - Thrive And Love 14

Eight - Cherish Your Presence 16

Nine - Giver Of Life 18

Ten - Humble And Towering 19

Eleven - Molecules Dance 21

Twelve - Intricate Dance 22

Thirteen - Expanse Of Sky 24

Fourteen - Blessing Widespread 26

Fifteen - Lifeblood Of Our Earth 28

Sixteen - Sustainer 30

Seventeen - Oceans Deep 31

Eighteen - Gardener's Prayer 33

Nineteen - Let Us Marvel 35

Twenty - The Nurturer 37

Twenty-One - Symphony Of Creation . . . 39

Twenty-Two - Soil To Sea 41

Twenty-Three - Essence 43

Twenty-Four - Vital Element 45

Twenty-Five - Invisible Yet Impactful . . . 47

Twenty-Six - Catalyst For Growth 49

Twenty-Seven - Vital Bonds 51

Twenty-Eight - Sacred Shrine 52

Twenty-Nine - Building Block 53

Thirty - Without Nitrogen 54

Thirty-One - Element Profound 56

Thirty-Two - Gift Of Abundance 58

Thirty-Three - Ebb And Tide	60
Thirty-Four - Catalyst Of Creation	62
Thirty-Five - Nitrogen, The Foundation	64
Thirty-Six - Connecting Us To God	66
Thirty-Seven - Birth To The End	68
Thirty-Eight - Harmonious Words	70
About The Author	72

WHY I CREATED THIS BOOK?

Creating a poetry book about the chemistry element of Nitrogen was an intriguing and unique endeavor. Nitrogen, as an element, possesses various qualities that can be metaphorically explored through poetry. Nitrogen is essential for life, found in proteins and DNA, and plays a vital role in the Earth's atmosphere. By incorporating scientific knowledge and imagery into poetry, I can create a fusion of art and science, captivating readers with a fresh perspective on the element. This book can not only educate readers about Nitrogen but also inspire them to appreciate the beauty of science and the natural world.

ONE

THE SILENT HERO

In the realm of elements, Nitrogen stands tall,
A silent force of nature, impacting us all.
With a symbol of N, it's electronegative,
Its atomic number, seven, is quite impressive.

In the atmosphere, it's abundant and free,
Making up most of the air we breathe.
A gas so essential, yet often overlooked,
Nitrogen, the element that keeps life hooked.

In the soil, it nourishes the plants,
Helping them grow with its magical chants.
A vital component of proteins and DNA,
Nitrogen, the building block of life's display.

From the lush green fields to the depths of the sea,
Nitrogen cycles, it moves ceaselessly.
From organism to organism, it transfers its might,
Fueling the circle of life, day and night.

In the laboratories, it takes on new forms,
Creating compounds, breaking norms.
From fertilizers to explosives, it plays its role,
Nitrogen, the versatile, with a powerful soul.

In the stars above, it shines so bright,
Forming molecules, a celestial delight.
The beauty of Nitrogen, so vast and grand,
A cosmic dance, orchestrated by its command.

So let us appreciate this element divine,
For its presence in our lives, so fine.
Nitrogen, the silent hero, we must adore,
For without it, life would be no more.

TWO

EVERY SPACE

In the realm of elements, there's one so pure,
A silent hero, always so secure.
From the air we breathe to the soil below,
Nitrogen, the vital essence, doth bestow.
    High above, it lingers in the azure sky,
Boundless and free, where birds and clouds do fly.
A tasteless gas, invisible, yet profound,
Nitrogen, a treasure that's always around.
    In the circle of life, it plays its part,
From plants to animals, it's found in every heart.
A building block of proteins, strong and true,
Nitrogen, the essence that renews.
    In the fields of green, where crops do grow,
It nourishes the Earth, a secret only farmers know.
For without this element, life would cease,
No food to eat, no beauty, no peace.

In the cosmos vast, where stars ignite,
Nitrogen shines, a celestial light.
From nebulae to galaxies, it's everywhere,
A cosmic dance, beyond compare.

Nitrogen, oh Nitrogen, we sing your praise,
For you're the essence that lights our days.
From the depths of the ocean to the highest peak,
Your presence is what we truly seek.

So let us marvel at this element divine,
For it's the foundation of life's grand design.
In every breath we take, we feel your grace,
Nitrogen, the element that fills every space.

THREE

HARMONIOUS WAYS

 In the realm of atoms, a noble gas,
Lies Nitrogen, with a beauty unsurpassed.
In the air, it reigns, invisible and pure,
A silent guardian, steadfast and sure.
 From the deepest oceans to the highest peaks,
Nitrogen's presence, the Earth gladly seeks.
It whispers through the leaves, dances in the rain,
Nourishing the soil, a life-giving domain.
 In the circle of life, it plays a vital role,
From the tiniest organisms to the mighty soul.
It weaves through the tapestry of nature's design,
A bond unbreakable, forever intertwined.
 Oh Nitrogen, you fill every space,
With your cosmic significance, you embrace.
From the birth of stars to the breath we take,
You're the foundation, the essence, the grandest stake.

So let us celebrate this element divine,
The giver of life, the elusive sign.
For Nitrogen, in all its forms, we praise,
A symphony of atoms, in harmonious ways.

FOUR

COSMIC EMBRACE

In the realm of skies, where stars ignite,
A cosmic dance, a celestial flight.
Amidst the vast expanse, where worlds align,
Lies the essence of Nitrogen, so divine.
   A breath of life, both humble and grand,
It weaves its magic across the land.
Through the verdant fields and forests deep,
Nitrogen nourishes, a promise to keep.
   From the heavens above to the soil below,
It circles through cycles, an eternal flow.
In the air we breathe, it whispers its song,
A symphony of life, steady and strong.
   It dances with plants, in symbiotic embrace,
Fueling their growth, with grace and with pace.
From seeds to blooms, it orchestrates the show,
A testament to Nitrogen's eternal glow.

In the rivers and streams, it finds its way,
Supporting creatures, in rivers that sway.
From the mighty whale to the tiniest fish,
Nitrogen sustains, a delectable dish.

And when the rain falls, in a gentle cascade,
Nitrogen mingles, in each droplet made.
It kisses the earth, with a tender touch,
Nurturing life, oh, how much it means so much.

So let us marvel, at Nitrogen's might,
A silent hero, in the day and the night.
For in its essence, we find our place,
Bound together, in cosmic embrace.

FIVE

PROTEINS AND DNA

In the realm of elements, let us explore,
A noble gas, Nitrogen, we adore.
In the air, it silently resides,
Nurturing plants, where life abides.
From the soil, it takes a vital role,
Assimilating in leaves, a green console.
A catalyst for growth, it does provide,
The nourishment plants need to survive.
In proteins and DNA, it finds its place,
A building block of life's intricate embrace.
From amino acids to enzymes so grand,
Nitrogen weaves creation's delicate strand.
In the circle of life, it dances its part,
From the smallest microbes to the beating heart.
A vital component, in every living cell,
Nitrogen's presence, we must always tell.

So let us cherish this element so pure,
For it sustains life, of that we are sure.
In the chemistry of nature, it plays its role,
Nitrogen, the essence that makes us whole.

SIX

OH, NITROGEN

In the heart of the Earth, where life begins,
There lies a secret, the essence within.
Nitrogen, the silent watcher of days,
Unseen, yet vital, in mysterious ways.

From the depths of the soil to the skies above,
Nitrogen dances, the bearer of love.
It breathes life into the lush green fields,
Where flowers bloom and nature yields.

In the air we breathe, it forms a bond,
With oxygen and carbon, a harmony spawned.
A gas so pure, it whispers in the breeze,
Nurturing life with gentle ease.

In the depths of the ocean, where creatures dwell,
Nitrogen weaves its magic spell.
It fuels the growth of coral reefs and kelp,
Where vibrant colors and life find help.

From the ancient forests to the deserts so dry,
Nitrogen whispers a lullaby.
It fuels the flames of the sun-soaked sand,
And paints the sky with hues so grand.
Oh, Nitrogen, the secret of life,
A dancer in harmony, free from strife.
In every molecule, in every breath,
You sustain us all, from birth to death.
So let us treasure this element divine,
For Nitrogen, the giver of life, shall forever shine.
In the tapestry of creation, woven with care,
Nitrogen, the unsung hero, always there.

SEVEN

THRIVE AND LOVE

In the cycle of life, a cosmic dance,
Nitrogen weaves its mysterious trance.
From the stars it descends, a celestial flight,
To nourish the Earth, bringing life's delight.
In the lofty skies, it floats with grace,
A gas so pure, embracing cosmic space.
In the atmosphere, its presence unseen,
Yet vital it is, in every living scene.
From the soil, it rises, a silent hero,
Fertilizing crops, making them grow.
Roots delve deep, seeking its embrace,
As plants reach up, towards the sun's warm face.
In the depths of the ocean, where life abounds,
Nitrogen swirls, in aquatic surrounds.
From tiny plankton to creatures grand,
It sustains them all, with its gentle hand.

In the forest, a symphony of green,
Nitrogen whispers, in every leaf's serene.
From towering trees to flowers fair,
It breathes life into the vibrant air.

In the nitrogen cycle, a delicate ballet,
It transforms, it shifts, in its graceful way.
From soil to plant, from plant to prey,
It travels on, in an eternal relay.

Nitrogen, a gift, from the cosmos above,
Essential it is, for life to thrive and love.
A silent force, in every living cell,
With every beat, its presence does tell.

So let us celebrate this humble element,
For without Nitrogen, life would be absent.
In the grand tapestry of nature's art,
Nitrogen weaves itself, in every part.

EIGHT

CHERISH YOUR PRESENCE

Nitrogen, a gas so pure,
Invisible, yet so secure,
It's in the air we breathe,
And in every living seed.

From the depths of the soil,
To the highest mountain foil,
Nitrogen nourishes the Earth,
Aiding in each life's birth.

From the cosmic dust it came,
Millions of years to claim,
A vital element in our universe,
A building block, a cosmic verse.

Nitrogen, oh how you sustain,
Life on this planet, without refrain,

From the smallest microbe,
To the largest blue whale's probe.
    In every molecule, you reside,
A precious element, never to hide,
Nitrogen, we cherish your presence,
For without you, there's no essence.

NINE

GIVER OF LIFE

In the depths of soil, where life takes root,
Nitrogen, the giver of strength, takes its route.
A silent partner, unseen, yet so vital,
Nourishing the earth, like a selfless recital.
　Through fixation, it finds its way,
From the air to the ground, without delay.
Legumes and bacteria, they hold the key,
Unlocking the nitrogen for all to see.
　From the leaves of green, to the roots down below,
Nitrogen dances, a graceful flow.
It weaves its magic, in every blade of grass,
Supporting life's tapestry, in a delicate mass.
　For without this element, the world would cease,
No growth, no sustenance, no inner peace.
So let us cherish Nitrogen, the giver of life,
A silent hero, in a world filled with strife.

TEN

HUMBLE AND TOWERING

In the tapestry of nature's design,
A thread of life, a breath divine,
There lies a element, pure and true,
Nitrogen, a sustainer through and through.
    Beneath the sky's cerulean hue,
Nitrogen whispers, secrets it imbues.
It weaves through soil, a silent tide,
Nourishing the Earth, where life abides.
    From tranquil fields of verdant green,
To mighty forests, nature's serene,
Nitrogen dances in the air,
A vital force, beyond compare.
    It binds the atoms, forms the bonds,
In proteins, DNA, where life responds.

With every beat, in every cell,
Nitrogen's melody, life's ancient spell.
   From humble seed to towering tree,
Nitrogen's touch, a symphony.
It fuels the growth, ignites the flame,
A catalyst for life, forever the same.
   So let us honor, with grateful hearts,
The role Nitrogen plays, a vital part.
For in its essence, we find the key,
To life's grand tapestry, eternally.

ELEVEN

MOLECULES DANCE

In every living cell, Nitrogen resides,
A vital element, life's secret guide.
From the depths of the soil to the heights of the sky,
Nitrogen's presence, we cannot deny.
    It fuels the growth of plants, tall and green,
In their leaves and stems, a thriving scene.
From roots to fruits, it's a constant friend,
Nitrogen's role, a cycle without end.
    In the air we breathe, Nitrogen is there,
A silent companion, beyond compare.
Its molecules dance, unseen and free,
A gift from nature, for you and me.
    So let us cherish this element divine,
Nitrogen's power, forever will shine.
In the tapestry of life, it weaves its thread,
A testament to its strength, in every spread.

TWELVE

INTRICATE DANCE

In the depths of soil, a silent force,
Nitrogen, the giver of life's course.
A catalyst for growth, it fuels the land,
Nourishing roots with its gentle hand.
From the humble seed to towering tree,
Nitrogen whispers, "Thrive, let it be."
It weaves through cells, a vital thread,
Enabling life to flourish, unfettered.
In chlorophyll's embrace, it dances and twirls,
Capturing sunlight, creating green swirls.
Photosynthesis sings, a symphony of grace,
With Nitrogen's touch, life finds its place.
In blooms of color and petals so fair,
Nitrogen's magic, suspended in the air.
A secret shared with the buzzing bee,
As pollen travels, life's grand decree.

From the mountains high to the oceans deep,
Nitrogen's presence, a promise to keep.
In the cycle of life, it plays its part,
A bond unbroken, a beating heart.

So let us celebrate this element true,
Nitrogen, the sustainer of life's debut.
From the tiniest cell to the vast expanse,
Its essence weaves nature's intricate dance.

THIRTEEN

EXPANSE OF SKY

In the realm of elements, Nitrogen stands tall,
A silent force, the giver of life to all.
Within its atoms, a power so grand,
A nourishing presence, across the land.
From the soil it rises, in plants it resides,
Fueling their growth, as life coincides.
From leafy greens to towering trees,
Nitrogen sustains, amidst the gentle breeze.
In every creature, in every cell,
Nitrogen weaves its magic spell.
Proteins and DNA, its building blocks,
Ensuring life's cycles never cease to unlock.
From the depths of the ocean to the vast expanse of sky,
Nitrogen dances, its purpose held high.

In the air we breathe, its presence unseen,
Yet vital for life, a constant routine.
    So let us marvel at Nitrogen's grace,
An element essential, in every space.
For without its touch, the world would be bare,
A reminder of the beauty it's destined to share.

FOURTEEN

BLESSING WIDESPREAD

In the soil beneath our feet, a hidden gift does lie,
A vital element, on which life does rely.
Nitrogen, the essence that nourishes the land,
An unseen force, in nature's intricate band.
From the air above, it silently descends,
Transforming barren fields into fertile lands.
Through lightning's crack and thunder's roar,
Nitrogen settles, enriching the core.
It binds with the Earth, in a delicate dance,
Feeding the roots, giving plants a chance.
From humble seed to towering tree,
Nitrogen fuels their growth, as far as the eye can see.
In the depths of the ocean, where life teems,
Nitrogen sustains, fulfilling its dreams.

From tiny plankton to majestic whales,
Nitrogen ensures life's grandest tales.
    So let us marvel at this element divine,
For without Nitrogen, life would surely decline.
In every breath we take, in every step we tread,
Nitrogen's presence, a blessing widespread.

FIFTEEN

LIFEBLOOD OF OUR EARTH

In fields of green and oceans deep,
Where life does grow and secrets keep,
There lies a force, a silent might,
A chemical element, pure and bright.
   Nitrogen, the giver of life,
Fueling growth amidst the strife,
From plant to beast, from sea to land,
Its presence vital, like a guiding hand.
   In molecules of air, it freely floats,
Nurturing the Earth with gentle notes,
Through roots and leaves, it finds its way,
Enriching soils, with each passing day.
   From humble seed to towering tree,
Nitrogen's touch, a symphony,

It weaves its magic, unseen, untold,
Transforming the barren into gold.

In the dance of life, it plays its part,
A catalyst for growth, a work of art,
With every breath we take, we owe,
Our gratitude to Nitrogen's flow.

So let us cherish this element rare,
In every breath, in every prayer,
For in its grace, we find our worth,
Nitrogen, the lifeblood of our Earth.

SIXTEEN

SUSTAINER

In fields of green, where life takes hold,
A silent hero, a story untold.
Nitrogen, the fuel beneath our feet,
Sustainer of growth, a symphony complete.
From the depths of soil, it rises high,
Nurturing plants that reach for the sky.
A catalyst for life, it breathes its might,
Fueling the dance of day and night.
Through bonds unseen, it weaves its spell,
In proteins and DNA, its secrets dwell.
From the tiniest microbes to the grandest trees,
Nitrogen whispers in life's symphony.
So let us honor this element so pure,
For without its touch, life would be obscure.
In every breath we take, it plays its part,
Nitrogen, the sustainer of life's art.

SEVENTEEN

OCEANS DEEP

In the realm of chemistry, there's a star so bright,
A vital element that fuels growth and might,
Nitrogen, oh Nitrogen, the breath of life it brings,
Sustaining every creature, the song that nature sings.

In the air we breathe, it dances with grace,
Forming bonds with others, in an elegant embrace,
It weaves through the atmosphere, a silent thread,
Nurturing the Earth, with every step we tread.

From the soil it rises, in plants it takes its form,
A catalyst for life, through the cycle it'll transform,
From roots to leaves, it orchestrates a grand ballet,
Fueling photosynthesis, in the sunlight's golden ray.

In blooms and petals, its magic does unfold,
Creating vibrant colors, a story yet untold,
With every gentle breeze, it whispers a sweet refrain,
Nitrogen, the secret behind nature's endless gain.

Within every creature, in every cell it dwells,
In proteins and DNA, its story softly tells,
A building block of life, it shapes us from within,
The essence of existence, where the journey begins.

So let us cherish Nitrogen, this element so rare,
For without its presence, life would be unfair,
From barren fields it transforms, to oceans deep and wide,
Sustaining life's dance, with love and grace beside.

In every breath we take, it nurtures our very core,
The lifeblood of our planet, forever we implore,
Nitrogen, oh Nitrogen, we honor your great role,
A symbol of resilience, forever in our soul.

EIGHTEEN

GARDENER'S PRAYER

In the depths of nature's breath,
Where life finds its eternal rest,
There lies a force, so pure and strong,
Nitrogen, the melody of life's song.
From the air, it silently descends,
Nurturing growth, where life extends,
It weaves its magic, unseen, untold,
A catalyst for wonders, manifold.
In the soil, it dances with delight,
Awakening seeds, taking flight,
Fueling the roots, with gentle care,
Nitrogen, the gardener's prayer.
From humble plants to towering trees,
It grants them strength, like gentle breeze,
With every leaf, every petal unfurled,
Nitrogen, the sustainer of this world.

Oh Nitrogen, we honor your grace,
In every step, every vibrant embrace,
For without your touch, life would cease,
A symphony of growth, eternal peace.

NINETEEN

LET US MARVEL

In fields once barren, a transformation begins,
As Nitrogen whispers, a dance it begins.
From soil to sky, its journey unfolds,
Nurturing growth with stories untold.
   A silent companion, it lingers unseen,
Yet vital to life, like a wellspring serene.
Through plants it courses, a vibrant tide,
Fueling the dance where life resides.
   In proteins and DNA, its presence abounds,
A building block of life profound.
From the depths of the sea to the highest peak,
Nitrogen's embrace, a language it speaks.
   It sustains the planet, a guardian true,
A giver of life, both old and anew.
From the smallest creature to the mightiest tree,
Nitrogen's touch, a lifeline to be.

So let us marvel at this element divine,
A catalyst for growth, both yours and mine.
In Nitrogen's presence, the world comes alive,
A symphony of wonders, forever to thrive.

TWENTY

THE NURTURER

In the realm of life, a silent dancer,
Nitrogen, the element, a hidden enhancer.
From the depths of soil, it gently rises,
Nurturing life, where barrenness disguises.
   A catalyst of growth, it breathes new life,
Transforming deserts into lands of rife.
It whispers to seeds, with a gentle touch,
Awakening the earth, it loves so much.
   Through symbiotic dance, it takes its place,
In the roots of plants, its essence they embrace.
Nitrogen, the nurturer, in a silent embrace,
Feeding the world with its tender grace.
   From the fields of green to the forests tall,
Nitrogen's presence, a gift to all.
It weaves through the fabric of every living thing,
An element essential, a symphony it sings.

Oh, Nitrogen, the giver of life's breath,
In air and soil, your presence we confess.
A humble element, yet mighty in its might,
Fueling growth and sustaining life's delight.

So, let us honor Nitrogen's sacred role,
In this dance of life, it plays a vital role.
For without its touch, this world we adore,
Would be barren and lifeless, forevermore.

TWENTY-ONE

SYMPHONY OF CREATION

In the realm of elements, a silent hero resides,
Nitrogen, the sustainer of growth, it abides.
Invisible to the eye, yet a force so profound,
It nurtures life's tapestry, on fertile ground.
From the depths of the soil to the vastness of air,
Nitrogen weaves its magic, with utmost care.
Through the roots it travels, a nourishing stream,
Fueling the green wonders, that on Earth gleam.
It dances with plants, in a delicate embrace,
Enriching their essence, with grace and embrace.
From leaves to stems, it lends its vibrant hue,
A symphony of life, ever-changing and true.
Nitrogen, the conductor of nature's grand choir,
Guiding the symphony, with a gentle desire.

In the cycle of life, it whispers its plea,
"Let growth be abundant, and harmony be."
   So let us honor this element, humble and pure,
For without Nitrogen, life would be obscure.
A silent hero, in the symphony of creation,
Nitrogen, the sustainer, our eternal foundation.

TWENTY-TWO

SOIL TO SEA

In the secret chambers of nature's reign,
There lies a power, hidden, yet untamed,
Nitrogen, the silent force that whispers,
Behind the scenes, where life finds its sustenance.
From Earth's core to the sky's expanse,
Nitrogen weaves its magic, a cosmic dance,
A catalyst for growth, a guardian of the land,
In every molecule, a gift, a helping hand.
It binds with carbon, oxygen, and more,
Creating life's tapestry, a symphony to adore,
From soil to sea, from flora to fauna,
Nitrogen's embrace, a gift from nirvana.
In the breath of plants, it fuels their might,
Green leaves shimmer under its gentle light,
From the depths of the ocean to the highest peak,
Nitrogen's touch, an enchantment we seek.

So, let us marvel at this elemental bliss,
Nitrogen, the giver of life's gentle kiss,
In the grand design, a secret, divine,
Nitrogen, the hidden thread that makes life shine.

TWENTY-THREE

ESSENCE

In the tapestry of life, a hidden thread,
A guardian of lands, where beauty's bred.
Nitrogen, the catalyst of growth,
Binds with elements, a symphony of hope.
    A silent force, beneath the soil's embrace,
Nurturing the roots with tender grace.
The giver of green, the fuel of might,
Nitrogen, the essence of life's true light.
    With every breath, we inhale its air,
A dance of atoms, beyond compare.
From the vast expanse of the starlit sky,
To the depths of oceans, where wonders lie.
    Nitrogen, the weaver, with an unseen hand,
Creating bonds, where life expands.
In proteins and DNA, its presence strong,
A building block, where resilience belongs.

From wheat fields swaying in the breeze,
To rainforests teeming with life's keys.
Nitrogen, the sustainer, in every leaf,
Whispering secrets, beyond belief.

Oh Nitrogen, how you endlessly inspire,
The symphony of life, where passions acquire.
In your embrace, the world finds its way,
A precious element, forever to stay.

So let us marvel at Nitrogen's might,
A guardian, a catalyst, shining so bright.
For in its essence, we truly find,
The essence of life, forever intertwined.

TWENTY-FOUR

VITAL ELEMENT

Nitrogen, oh Nitrogen, an element so dear,
A silent hero, ever-present, without any fear.
From the soil to the sky, you play a vital role,
Fueling growth and sustaining life, a conductor of the whole.

In the air, you form a blanket, protecting from the sun,
And in the water, you're the source of life, where it all begun.
You're a part of every cell, every living being,
A key component of DNA, the code of our being.

But there's more to you, Nitrogen, than meets the eye,
You're a catalyst for growth, a force that can't be denied.

You help create the bonds, that hold life together,
Inspiring the symphony of life, that lasts forever.
 Nitrogen, oh Nitrogen, you may be invisible,
But your impact on life, is truly incredible.
So here's to you, Nitrogen, the unsung hero of the land,
A vital element, that we all need to understand.

TWENTY-FIVE

INVISIBLE YET IMPACTFUL

In the realm of nature's embrace,
A giver of life, with gentle grace.
Nitrogen, the element divine,
Nurturing souls, like an ancient wine.

Through boundless fields and meadows wide,
It weaves a tapestry, side by side.
From lush green leaves to towering trees,
Nitrogen whispers in the gentle breeze.

In the soil, it lies, a silent friend,
Fueling growth, from beginning to end.
It binds the atoms, a conductor's role,
Nature's symphony, a harmonious whole.

From the depths of oceans to the starry skies,
Nitrogen dances, as life's ally.

It fuels the flame, ignites the spark,
In every living thing, leaves a mark.
 A catalyst for growth, it takes its flight,
Unseen, yet present, in day and night.
Guardian of the land, it stands tall,
Holding the essence of life in its thrall.
 From the smallest seed to the mightiest tree,
Nitrogen's touch, a lifeline, you see.
It creates the bonds that hold life together,
In every living being, now and forever.
 So let us celebrate this noble guest,
For Nitrogen's gift, we are truly blessed.
A nurturer, a giver, a guardian, a friend,
Invisible yet impactful, till the very end.

TWENTY-SIX

CATALYST FOR GROWTH

In the realm of elements, Nitrogen stands tall,
A catalyst for growth, it nurtures one and all.
With a gentle touch, it breathes life into the land,
A guardian of nature, a steady guiding hand.
    From the soil it rises, in a dance with the air,
Embracing the roots, with a bond beyond compare.
It whispers to the plants, a secret of their worth,
Fueling their existence, giving beauty its birth.
    In the sky, it lingers, in a cloak of blue,
A silent sentinel, watching all that we do.
It weaves through the clouds, in a celestial flight,
A guardian of the atmosphere, protecting us with might.
    Oh, Nitrogen, element of grace and might,
You shape the world, both in darkness and light.

A catalyst for growth, a guardian of the land,
In your presence, life flourishes, hand in hand.

TWENTY-SEVEN

VITAL BONDS

In the realm of elements, Nitrogen stands tall,
A guardian of the land, it answers nature's call.
Deep within the soil, its presence is felt,
A catalyst for growth, where life is truly dwelt.

From the mighty trees to the humblest of plants,
Nitrogen nourishes, with its magical chants.
It binds with other elements, forming vital bonds,
Fueling the cycle of life, where harmony responds.

In the air, it floats, a silent guardian above,
Protecting life below with a gentle love.
In every breath we take, Nitrogen is there,
Sustaining our existence, with utmost care.

So let us celebrate Nitrogen, the element divine,
A catalyst for growth, in nature's grand design.
With its presence felt, in every living thing,
Nitrogen, the guardian, forever shall sing.

TWENTY-EIGHT

SACRED SHRINE

In the realm of elements, a noble star,
Nitrogen, the catalyst from afar.
A guardian of the land, it does bestow,
A force of growth, where life shall ever flow.

With gentle touch, it stirs the soil's embrace,
Awakening dormant seeds, with tender grace.
Through symbiotic dance, it forms a bond,
With plants and microbes, forever beyond.

A giver of green, a sustainer of life,
Nitrogen, the protector in the strife.
From the breath of stars, it holds the key,
To nature's beauty, and harmony's decree.

So let us honor this element divine,
For it sustains us, like a sacred shrine.
In the cycle of life, it plays its part,
Nitrogen, the guardian of every heart.

TWENTY-NINE

BUILDING BLOCK

In the realm of elements, Nitrogen stands tall,
A catalyst for growth, it answers the call.
With a silent presence, it permeates the air,
Fueling life's cycles, with utmost care.
From the depths of the soil to the highest tree,
Nitrogen's touch, a gift to see.
It binds with the roots, like a guardian true,
Nurturing the land, where life can ensue.
In the dance of creation, it plays its part,
A building block of proteins, from the start.
In every living cell, it weaves its thread,
A foundation of life, where dreams are bred.
Nitrogen, the silent hero of the land,
Sustaining ecosystems with a gentle hand.
With every breath we take, its essence flows,
A lifeline for nature, that forever grows.

THIRTY

WITHOUT NITROGEN

In nature's realm, a guardian stands tall,
A steadfast force, the guardian of all.
Nitrogen, the element of the air,
With unseen might, it tends to nature's care.

A steady guiding hand, it leads the way,
Through cycles of growth, day after day.
From soil to plant, it fosters life's bloom,
A catalyst for growth, dispelling gloom.

In roots it dwells, a silent embrace,
Nourishing the earth with its gentle grace.
Through enzymes and proteins, it plays its part,
Fueling life's cycles, a work of art.

From the depths of soil to the open sky,
Nitrogen's presence, we can't deny.
A guardian of the land, it will remain,
A protector in the cycle of life's refrain.

So let us honor this element true,
For without nitrogen, what would life pursue?
A force of growth, a sustainer of green,
In its essence, the beauty of life is seen.

THIRTY-ONE

ELEMENT PROFOUND

In the realm of elements, Nitrogen stands tall,
A catalyst for growth, it nurtures us all.
Guardian of the land, it silently resides,
Invisible yet essential, where life abides.
It dances through the soil, a gentle embrace,
Enriching every root, with its tender grace.
From lush green meadows to forests so grand,
Nitrogen's touch paints landscapes across the land.
It whispers to the seeds, a promise it makes,
To awaken their dreams, and quench their thirst's ache.
From the tallest trees to the tiniest bloom,
Nitrogen's presence ensures life will resume.
A guardian, a nurturer, this element profound,
Nitrogen's gifts in abundance can be found.

With every breath we take, we owe our thanks,
To Nitrogen's role in life's eternal dance.

THIRTY-TWO

GIFT OF ABUNDANCE

In the realm of atoms and compounds so grand,
There lies a noble element, Nitrogen, as it stands.
A catalyst for growth, a guardian of the land,
It weaves its magic, with a gentle hand.
From the skies above, it silently descends,
Nourishing the earth, where life transcends.
In the soil, it dances, with microbes it blends,
Fueling the cycle, where vitality never ends.
In the greenest fields, where crops sway,
Nitrogen whispers secrets, day by day.
With every breath of life, it finds its way,
Enriching the roots, in a mystical display.
From the mighty oak to the humble fern,
Nitrogen courses through, a lesson to learn.
It builds the proteins, that make life burn,
A vital component, at every twist and turn.

Oh Nitrogen, the silent hero of the land,
Sustaining life with a touch so grand.
In the chemistry of nature, you take a stand,
A gift of abundance, forever in demand.

THIRTY-THREE

EBB AND TIDE

In the realm where elements reside,
A silent guardian does preside.
Nitrogen, noble and true,
Fuels growth and sustains life too.
In the air, it lingers unseen,
Invisible, yet so serene.
A vital force, it does bestow,
To all that live, to all that grow.
Within the soil, it finds its home,
Nurturing the land, where seeds are sown.
From humble roots to towering trees,
Nitrogen's touch whispers with ease.
It dances with carbon, hand in hand,
Creating life's intricate strand.
From amino acids to proteins vast,
Nitrogen weaves its magic, unsurpassed.

In the ocean's depths, it does reside,
Fostering life, with the ebb and tide.
From coral reefs to creatures deep,
Nitrogen's embrace, their secrets keep.

So let us praise this element divine,
For its role in nature's grand design.
Nitrogen, a silent guardian so true,
Fueling growth and sustaining life anew.

THIRTY-FOUR

CATALYST OF CREATION

In the heart of air, a silent hero lies,
A giver of life, beneath vast skies.
Nitrogen, oh noble element of Earth,
A force unseen, yet of immeasurable worth.
From atmosphere to soil, you gently flow,
Sustaining ecosystems, making life grow.
A chemical bond, with oxygen united,
Fueling growth, from the depths to the heighted.
In plants, you journey through their roots,
Nurturing the soil with your precious fruits.
From green leaves to vibrant blooms,
You bring color to nature's rooms.
In the oceans, you dance with the waves,
Supporting life in your invisible embrace.

From tiny plankton to mighty whales,
You're the essence of life's grand tale.
    Nitrogen, you're the catalyst of creation,
An element of wonder and admiration.
In every breath we take, you're there,
A vital presence, beyond compare.

THIRTY-FIVE

NITROGEN, THE FOUNDATION

In the realm of elements, a star does shine,
Nitrogen, the giver of life divine.
Amidst the heavens, its atoms dance,
A cosmic ballet, a fortunate chance.
From the depths of space, it found its way,
To Earth's embrace, where life holds sway.
In the air we breathe, it quietly resides,
Fueling growth, where hope abides.
In the fields, it weaves its magic thread,
Nurturing crops, where abundance is spread.
From the tiniest seed to towering trees,
Nitrogen whispers life's symphonies.
Through the rivers and lakes, it gently flows,
Nourishing creatures, where its essence bestows.

From the bustling cities to the tranquil shores,
Nitrogen's presence, each life adores.

In the cycle of life, it plays its part,
A silent hero, never to depart.
From birth to death, it sustains us all,
Nitrogen, the foundation, standing tall.

So let us honor this element grand,
With gratitude, we shall forever stand.
For Nitrogen's gift, abundant and true,
Fueling life's journey, in all that we do.

THIRTY-SIX

CONNECTING US TO GOD

In the depths of the earth, Nitrogen dwells,
A guardian of the land, its story it tells.
Silent and steady, beneath the soil it resides,
Enriching every root, where life quietly hides.

It binds the atoms, with a powerful force,
Creating compounds, a chemical discourse.
From proteins to DNA, it weaves its magic,
A vital component, essential and tragic.

In the air, it floats, a vast ocean above,
Fueling the cycle of life with its love.
From plants to animals, from sea to sky,
Nitrogen dances, never asking why.

It joins the chorus, in nature's grand design,
Creating harmony, a symphony so fine.

From the smallest microbe, to the mightiest tree,
Nitrogen's presence, a gift for all to see.
    It sustains life, with an invisible hand,
Nurturing ecosystems, across every land.
From the depths of the ocean, to the highest peak,
Nitrogen's embrace, forever we seek.
    So let us cherish this element divine,
For Nitrogen's gift is truly sublime.
In every breath we take, in every step we trod,
Nitrogen is the lifeline, connecting us to God.

THIRTY-SEVEN

BIRTH TO THE END

In the vast expanse where life takes its course,
There lies an element, Nitrogen, a force.
With a power unseen, yet so profound,
It nurtures life in every corner, all around.

Deep in the soil, where roots entwine,
Nitrogen whispers, a secret divine.
It fuels the growth of plants so green,
Creating a world of beauty, yet unseen.

From fields of wheat to towering trees,
Nitrogen dances in the gentle breeze.
It weaves its magic, a vital thread,
Supporting life, as it's widely spread.

In the depths of the ocean, where creatures hide,
Nitrogen thrives, an ally by their side.
From tiny plankton to majestic whales,
It sustains their existence, as their story unveils.

In the air we breathe, Nitrogen soars high,
A giver of life, it touches the sky.
It forms the very fabric of our being,
A silent hero, forever all-seeing.

Oh, Nitrogen, we sing your praise,
For your abundant and essential ways.
You nurture life, from birth to the end,
A cherished companion, our eternal friend.

THIRTY-EIGHT

HARMONIOUS WORDS

In the realm of atoms, a silent hero resides,
A giver of life, where beauty abides.
Nitrogen, the element of the air,
Nurturing life with tender care.
In the depths of soil, where roots entwine,
Nitrogen enriches, a gift divine.
From the smallest seed to towering trees,
It fuels their growth and sets them free.
In the ocean's depths, where creatures roam,
Nitrogen dances, a vital tome.
From tiny plankton to majestic whales,
It supports life's web, in intricate trails.
From the buzzing bees to the soaring birds,
Nitrogen connects, in harmonious words.
Through the cycles of nature, it gracefully weaves,
A symphony of life, that forever achieves.

So let us celebrate this mighty force,
For Nitrogen's gift, our lives endorse.
In every breath we take, in every beat of our hearts,
Nitrogen, the essence, that never departs.

ABOUT THE AUTHOR

Walter the Educator is one of the pseudonyms for Walter Anderson. Formally educated in Chemistry, Business, and Education, he is an educator, an author, a diverse entrepreneur, and he is the son of a disabled war veteran. "Walter the Educator" shares his time between educating and creating. He holds interests and owns several creative projects that entertain, enlighten, enhance, and educate, hoping to inspire and motivate you.

Follow, find new works, and stay up to date with Walter the Educator™ at WaltertheEducator.com

www.ingramcontent.com/pod-product-compliance
Lightning Source LLC
LaVergne TN
LVHW010602070526
838199LV00063BA/5050